# AI Ethics Foundations

## Understanding Moral Responsibility in Intelligent Machines

*By Joe Correa*

Published by Live Stronger Faster



First Edition

# Table of Contents

# Overview

Artificial intelligence has crossed a threshold that few people fully understand. What was once a laboratory curiosity or a narrow technical tool has now become a force that influences who gets hired, who receives a loan, who is flagged by law enforcement, what medical treatment a patient receives, and even what information entire societies believe to be true. Algorithms now make decisions that directly shape human lives, often faster, broader, and with more authority than any individual human ever could. Yet unlike human decision-makers, these systems do not possess conscience, empathy, or moral intuition. They execute instructions written in code, trained on data that reflects human history in all its brilliance and all its injustice. This reality makes one question unavoidable: when machines make decisions that affect people, who is morally responsible for the outcomes?

AI ethics exists because technology has reached a point where it can no longer be treated as neutral. Every algorithm contains values, whether intentional or not. When a facial recognition system misidentifies a person, when a loan-approval model denies credit, or when an automated hiring tool filters out certain candidates, these are not just technical errors; they are ethical events. They carry real-world consequences such as lost opportunities, discrimination, financial harm, and erosion of trust in institutions. As artificial intelligence spreads across every industry, the question is no longer whether ethics matter in AI, but how ethics can be embedded deeply enough to govern machines that now operate at a global scale.

This book is the foundation of a larger professional series because ethical questions come before legal compliance, technical design, or corporate policy. Laws are always reactive, written after damage has already occurred. Ethics, by contrast, is proactive. It asks what should be built, not merely what is allowed. It forces organizations, engineers, regulators, and executives to confront the human impact of their technologies before harm becomes unavoidable. Without ethical grounding, AI governance becomes little more than a bureaucratic exercise, focused on checklists and paperwork rather than the deeper responsibility of protecting human dignity.

One of the most profound challenges of AI ethics is the shifting nature of responsibility. In traditional systems, it was clear who was accountable when something went wrong. A doctor made a diagnosis, a banker approved a loan, or a judge made a ruling. With AI, decisions are often made by complex models that no single person fully understands. These systems learn patterns from massive datasets, adjusting themselves in ways even their creators cannot always predict. When such a system makes a harmful decision, is the blame assigned to the programmer, the company, the data provider, the user, or the machine itself? AI ethics begins by answering this question clearly: moral responsibility always remains with humans, even when decisions are automated.

The myth of the "objective algorithm" has done enormous damage. Many organizations assume that because a machine produces an output, it must be fair, unbiased, or scientifically neutral. In reality, algorithms inherit the values, assumptions, and historical inequalities embedded in their training data. If an AI system is trained on biased hiring data, it will reproduce discriminatory hiring patterns. If it is trained on biased lending data, it will amplify financial exclusion. The machine does not create injustice on its own; it reflects the injustice already present in the world. AI ethics exists to identify these hidden value systems and make them visible, so they can be challenged, corrected, and governed.

Transparency sits at the heart of ethical AI. People have a fundamental right to understand how decisions that affect their lives are made. When a human denies a loan, that decision can be questioned, appealed, and explained. When an algorithm does the same, the reasoning may be buried inside millions or billions of parameters that no human can directly interpret. This creates a dangerous imbalance of power. Ethical AI demands that systems be explainable, auditable, and open to challenge, even when they are technically complex. A decision that cannot be explained is not just a technical problem; it is a moral one.

Data is the fuel of artificial intelligence, but it is also deeply personal. Every medical record, financial transaction, social media post, and biometric scan represents a piece of someone's life. When organizations collect and use this data, they are not just handling information; they are handling human identity. Ethical AI requires informed consent, meaningful control, and respect for privacy. It rejects the idea that people are merely data sources to be harvested and monetized. Instead, it treats individuals as rights-bearing participants in the digital ecosystem.

As AI becomes embedded in governments, corporations, healthcare systems, financial institutions, and law enforcement, ethical failures scale at terrifying speed. A biased human might harm dozens of people in a career; a biased algorithm can harm millions in a matter of weeks. This is why ethics cannot be optional. It must be institutionalized through governance frameworks, accountability structures, and global standards. Ethical AI is not about slowing innovation; it is about ensuring that innovation does not undermine democracy, fairness, or human rights.

This book will guide you through the philosophical, legal, and practical foundations of AI ethics. You will learn what AI ethics truly means, how responsibility should be assigned between humans and machines, how bias arises and spreads through algorithms, why transparency is essential, and how accountability must be enforced. You will explore global standards, regulatory principles, and the real-world cost of unethical AI. Most importantly, you will gain the intellectual tools needed to evaluate any AI system, regardless of industry or application, through an ethical lens.

The future will not be shaped by artificial intelligence alone. It will be shaped by the values we encode into it. Every dataset, every model, every line of code is a moral choice, whether acknowledged or not. By understanding AI ethics at a foundational level, you are not just learning about technology; you are learning how to protect people in an increasingly automated world. This book marks the beginning of that responsibility, and it will prepare you for the deeper legal, technical, and governance challenges explored throughout the rest of this professional series.

*Chapter 1*

# What Is AI Ethics and Why It Matters

Artificial intelligence ethics is the discipline that examines how intelligent machines should be designed, deployed, governed, and controlled so that they serve humanity rather than harm it. Unlike traditional software, AI does not simply follow fixed instructions; it learns from data, adapts to new situations, and makes decisions that affect real people. This makes AI fundamentally different from earlier technologies. A spreadsheet cannot deny a mortgage. A word processor cannot diagnose cancer. But an AI system can do both. AI ethics exists because we have created machines that now participate in decision-making domains that were once reserved exclusively for human judgment.

At its core, AI ethics is about power. AI systems concentrate enormous power in the hands of those who build and control them. A small group of engineers or corporations can influence millions of lives through a single algorithm. When an AI model determines who gets a job interview, who qualifies for credit, or who is flagged as suspicious by law enforcement, it is exercising power over human opportunity and freedom. Ethical AI demands that this power be constrained by fairness, transparency, accountability, and respect for human rights.

One of the most dangerous misconceptions about AI is that it is neutral. Machines are often perceived as more objective than humans, but in reality they are shaped by human choices at every stage of their creation. Developers choose what data to collect. Organizations decide what outcomes to optimize. Executives decide where the system will be deployed. These choices embed values into the algorithm long before it ever produces a result. AI ethics exists to make these hidden values visible and to ensure they align with societal standards of justice and dignity.

Ethics also becomes essential because AI systems scale mistakes at unprecedented speed. A biased human manager might unfairly reject dozens of applicants over years. A biased hiring algorithm can reject thousands of qualified candidates in days. The magnitude of harm grows with automation. This means even small ethical flaws can produce enormous social damage. AI ethics therefore focuses not just on preventing intentional wrongdoing, but also on detecting and correcting unintended harm that arises from complex systems interacting with real-world data.

Another critical dimension of AI ethics is autonomy. As AI becomes more advanced, systems are given more freedom to act without human oversight. Self-driving cars decide how to react in emergencies. Trading algorithms move billions of dollars in milliseconds. Medical AI recommends treatments that affect survival. When machines operate with this level of autonomy, ethical safeguards must be embedded directly into their design. Otherwise, society risks surrendering moral decision-making to systems that do not understand the consequences of their actions.

Trust is the currency of the digital age. People must trust that AI systems are not secretly manipulating them, discriminating against them, or exploiting their data. Without trust, public backlash, regulation, and legal action will slow or halt technological progress. Ethical AI builds trust by ensuring that systems are transparent, explainable, and accountable. When people understand how a decision was made and who is responsible for it, they are far more likely to accept its outcome.

AI ethics also intersects with global inequality. Most AI systems are built in wealthy countries using data from specific populations, yet they are deployed worldwide. This creates a risk that technology designed for one group will harm or exclude others. Ethical AI requires that systems be tested, audited, and adapted for diverse cultures, languages, and socioeconomic conditions. It rejects the idea that one model can fairly serve all humanity without careful governance. Legal systems are now racing to catch up with artificial intelligence, but ethics must lead the way. Laws define what is forbidden; ethics defines what is right. Companies that rely only on legal compliance will always be one scandal away from disaster. Those that build ethical responsibility into their AI systems will not only avoid harm, but will also gain long-term competitive advantage through trust, stability, and public confidence.

In the coming decades, artificial intelligence will influence nearly every aspect of human life. Whether this influence is beneficial or destructive depends on how well ethical principles are integrated into technology from the start. AI ethics is not an abstract philosophy. It is the practical framework that determines whether intelligent machines become tools of empowerment or instruments of control.

*"The Algorithm That Knew Too Much"*

When Elena first noticed something was wrong, it was a single rejected loan application. Then another. Then a hundred more. As the lead data analyst at a fast-growing fintech company, she monitored approval rates daily. One morning, the numbers had shifted in a way that made her stomach tighten. Applicants from certain zip codes were suddenly being denied at nearly twice the previous rate. The algorithm, praised by executives as "perfectly objective," was quietly drawing invisible lines through entire communities. At first, Elena assumed it was a data glitch. She ran tests, reloaded datasets, and checked for coding errors. Everything looked clean. The model was working exactly as designed. That was what terrified her. The system was not broken. It was simply following the patterns it had learned from historical data—data shaped by decades of discriminatory lending practices. The machine was not inventing bias. It was preserving it with mathematical precision.

When Elena raised her concerns to management, she was told not to worry. “The algorithm is neutral,” her supervisor said. “It only sees numbers.” But Elena knew that numbers could lie. Behind every data point was a person with a story, a family, and a future. Each denial meant a business that would not open, a home that would not be bought, a child who would grow up in a different neighborhood.

Unable to let it go, Elena built a shadow model on her own time. She removed certain historical variables and introduced fairness constraints. The results shocked her. Approval rates rose without increasing default risk. The company could make the same profits without destroying opportunity for thousands of people. The harm was not necessary. It was simply invisible.

When Elena presented her findings to the executive board, the room fell silent. The algorithm had been boosting short-term profit by quietly excluding entire populations. No law had been broken. No regulation had been violated. Yet something was deeply wrong. For the first time, the leadership realized that their machine was making moral choices they had never authorized.

They faced a decision: continue using a system that maximized profit while deepening inequality, or redesign it to serve both business and humanity. It was not a technical choice. It was an ethical one. And for the first time in the company's history, an algorithm was no longer just a tool—it was a mirror reflecting who they truly were.

Elena left the meeting unsure of what the board would decide, but she knew one thing for certain. Artificial intelligence had forced them to confront a truth that could no longer be ignored. Machines may not have morals, but the people who build them always do.

*Chapter 2*

# Human vs. Machine Responsibility

As artificial intelligence becomes increasingly embedded in decision-making systems, one of the most urgent ethical questions facing society is deceptively simple: when something goes wrong, who is responsible? In traditional systems, responsibility is clearly assigned to a human being. A doctor makes a diagnosis, a banker approves a loan, a judge issues a sentence. With AI, those lines blur. Decisions are now made by machines trained on vast datasets and optimized by mathematical functions that no single person can fully understand. Yet despite this complexity, moral and legal responsibility cannot be delegated to software. Machines may execute decisions, but humans design, deploy, and authorize them.

The idea that AI might be "at fault" for harmful outcomes is seductive because it seems to remove blame from people. When an algorithm discriminates, denies services, or causes harm, organizations often say the system made a mistake. This language subtly shifts accountability away from human actors. In ethical terms, this is unacceptable. An algorithm does not choose its goals, its training data, or its operating environment. Those choices are made by engineers, executives, vendors, and regulators. AI ethics demands that responsibility remain firmly anchored in human hands, no matter how automated a process becomes.

One of the greatest dangers of advanced AI is what scholars call moral distancing. When decisions are automated, people feel less emotionally connected to the consequences. A loan officer who denies credit to a family may feel discomfort or doubt. An algorithm does not. Worse, the human managers overseeing the system may never see the individual cases affected by their technology. This distance makes it easier to tolerate harm, because no one feels personally responsible for it. Ethical governance requires structures that force human oversight, review, and accountability back into automated processes.

The complexity of modern AI systems creates another challenge: even developers may not fully understand how a model reaches a particular decision. Machine learning models adjust millions or billions of internal parameters during training, creating patterns that cannot easily be explained. This technical opacity can tempt organizations to claim ignorance when harm occurs. But ethical responsibility does not depend on perfect understanding. If a company deploys a system that it cannot explain, it still bears full responsibility for the outcomes that system produces. This principle is already embedded in many areas of society. Manufacturers are responsible for products even if a failure is caused by a complex interaction of components. Doctors are responsible for treatments even when outcomes are uncertain. In the same way, organizations that deploy AI are responsible for its behavior. Ethical AI requires rigorous testing, monitoring, and auditing to ensure that systems behave within acceptable boundaries. It also requires clear lines of accountability so that when harm occurs, victims know where to seek redress.

The idea of shared responsibility is also central to AI ethics. No single actor creates or controls an AI system. Data providers, model developers, cloud providers, and end users all play a role. Ethical governance requires that responsibility be distributed across this entire chain. A vendor cannot hide behind a customer, and a customer cannot hide behind a vendor. Each participant must take ownership of the part they play in shaping the system's behavior.

As AI systems become more autonomous, the temptation to treat them as independent agents will grow. Self-driving cars, automated trading systems, and autonomous weapons all operate with minimal human intervention. But autonomy does not equal moral agency. A machine can optimize for speed or profit, but it cannot understand justice, compassion, or human dignity. Ethical frameworks must ensure that meaningful human control remains in place, especially in high-risk applications.

Ultimately, the question of human versus machine responsibility is not about technology. It is about whether society will allow power to escape accountability. AI ethics insists that every automated decision be traceable back to human choices. Only by preserving this link can we ensure that intelligent machines remain tools of human values rather than forces beyond our control.

*"Who Signed the Code?"*

The accident happened in less than a second. A self-driving delivery vehicle swerved to avoid a falling branch and struck a cyclist on a quiet city street. The woman survived, but her injuries were severe. Within hours, news crews gathered, lawyers issued statements, and the company behind the vehicle released a carefully worded apology. The software, they said, had made a split-second decision based on safety protocols. No one had done anything wrong.

Marcus, the engineer who had helped write those safety protocols, sat alone in his office staring at the code on his screen. He recognized the decision path immediately. The system had been trained to prioritize vehicle occupants over pedestrians when collision probabilities exceeded a certain threshold. It had done exactly what it was designed to do. Yet a human being lay in a hospital bed because of that design choice.

In the days that followed, the company's executives insisted the algorithm was to blame. Regulators struggled to assign liability. The software vendor pointed to the hardware manufacturer. The manufacturer pointed to the data scientists. Everyone pointed somewhere else. The machine, silent and indifferent, became a convenient shield behind which everyone hid.

Marcus could not accept that. He knew that the algorithm did not choose its priorities. He and his team had. They had debated those thresholds, tested those scenarios, and signed off on those parameters. The machine had no conscience, but he did. When he finally spoke up in a closed-door meeting, his voice shook as he said, "The code didn't make this decision. We did."

That sentence changed everything. It forced the company to confront a truth they had been avoiding. Automation had not erased responsibility. It had only made it easier to forget. And for Marcus, that realization would never leave him, no matter how advanced the machines became.

*Chapter 3*

# Algorithmic Bias Explained as Systems

Algorithmic bias occurs when an artificial intelligence system produces systematically unfair outcomes for certain groups of people. These biases are not random errors; they are patterns of unequal treatment that arise from the data, design choices, and objectives embedded in a model. Because AI systems learn from historical information, they inherit the inequalities, prejudices, and distortions that exist in the real world. When these systems are deployed at scale, they do not merely reflect bias—they amplify it, turning yesterday's injustices into tomorrow's automated policies.

The most common source of algorithmic bias is training data. AI models learn by analyzing large datasets and identifying correlations. If those datasets reflect discriminatory hiring practices, unequal policing, or biased lending decisions, the model will internalize those patterns as if they were neutral truths. For example, a hiring algorithm trained on decades of company data may learn that certain demographics were historically hired less often, and it may treat that pattern as evidence of lower suitability. The model does not know that discrimination caused the pattern; it simply learns that the pattern exists.

Bias can also enter through problem framing. When developers define what an AI system is supposed to optimize, they make value judgments about what matters. A loan model optimized purely for minimizing defaults may exclude entire communities that have been historically denied financial stability. A policing algorithm optimized for arrest rates may disproportionately target neighborhoods that were already over-policed. Ethical AI requires questioning not only how a system works, but what it is designed to maximize.

Another hidden source of bias lies in feature selection. AI models do not see people; they see variables. Age, zip code, education level, browsing history, and hundreds of other data points are used to make predictions. Some of these variables act as proxies for protected characteristics such as race, gender, or income. Even if a model is not explicitly told someone's race, it may infer it through correlated data. This makes discrimination harder to detect and easier to deny.

The danger of algorithmic bias is not limited to any one industry. It appears in healthcare when diagnostic tools perform poorly on underrepresented populations. It appears in finance when credit models deny loans to certain groups. It appears in criminal justice when risk assessment tools overestimate the likelihood of reoffending for specific demographics. In each case, the harm is magnified by the authority of technology. People are more likely to accept an unfair decision when it is delivered by a machine.

Detecting bias requires rigorous testing and auditing. Models must be evaluated across different demographic groups to identify disparities in error rates, outcomes, and treatment. Ethical AI does not assume fairness; it measures it. This requires access to sensitive demographic data, careful statistical analysis, and a willingness to confront uncomfortable truths about how systems actually behave.

Correcting bias is not simply a technical challenge; it is a moral one. Developers may need to rebalance datasets, change optimization goals, or introduce fairness constraints that reduce overall accuracy in order to produce more equitable outcomes. These trade-offs force organizations to decide whether efficiency is more important than justice. AI ethics insists that human dignity cannot be sacrificed for marginal gains in performance.

Ultimately, algorithmic bias reveals a deeper truth about artificial intelligence: it is a mirror of society. If we feed machines a world shaped by inequality, they will learn inequality. Ethical AI requires not just better code, but a commitment to fairness, inclusion, and accountability at every stage of development and deployment.

*"The Pattern in the Data"*

Nina had spent her career trusting numbers. As a data scientist for a global healthcare company, she believed that statistics told the truth when people could not. So when the new diagnostic AI was rolled out, she was confident it would improve patient outcomes. The model had been trained on millions of medical records and promised unprecedented accuracy. Doctors began relying on it almost immediately.

It was a junior analyst who noticed the first anomaly. Patients from certain neighborhoods were being flagged as lower priority for advanced treatments. At first, the difference seemed small. Then it grew. Nina dug into the data and discovered a disturbing pattern. The model was learning from historical treatment records that reflected decades of unequal access to healthcare. Communities that had received less care in the past were now being deemed less worthy of care in the future.

The algorithm had found a pattern, but it was not a medical truth. It was a social scar. Yet the machine could not tell the difference. To it, lower treatment rates looked like lower medical need. The result was a feedback loop that quietly denied resources to the people who needed them most.

When Nina presented her findings, some executives argued that changing the model would reduce efficiency. The system was doing what it was designed to do: optimize outcomes based on past data. But Nina knew that past data was not neutral. It was shaped by injustice. Leaving the model unchanged would not just reflect inequality—it would harden it into policy.

Late one night, Nina rewrote the training process. She introduced fairness constraints and reweighted the data. The model became slightly less accurate by traditional metrics, but vastly more equitable. When the new version went live, treatment recommendations became balanced across communities.

No press release announced the change. Most patients would never know it happened. But Nina did. And she knew that sometimes the most important ethical victories are the ones written quietly into the code.

*Chapter 4*

# Transparency vs. Trade Secrets in AI Ethics

One of the central tensions in AI ethics lies between transparency and trade secrets. On one side is the ethical demand that people understand how decisions affecting their lives are made. On the other side is the business reality that companies protect their algorithms as valuable intellectual property. This conflict sits at the heart of nearly every debate about artificial intelligence governance. Transparency is essential for accountability, fairness, and trust, yet secrecy is often justified in the name of innovation and competitive advantage.

Transparency in AI means more than simply disclosing that a machine made a decision. It requires that the logic, data sources, and performance characteristics of a system be accessible to those who are affected by it. If an algorithm denies someone a mortgage or flags them as a fraud risk, that person should have the right to know why. Without this insight, individuals are powerless to challenge errors, bias, or abuse. Ethical AI therefore treats explanation as a fundamental right, not a luxury. Trade secrets complicate this principle. Many AI models represent years of research, millions of dollars in investment, and a company's core competitive advantage. Businesses fear that exposing how their systems work will allow competitors to copy them or bad actors to exploit them. These concerns are not trivial. However, protecting intellectual property cannot justify hiding harmful or discriminatory behavior. Ethical governance must strike a balance between protecting innovation and protecting people.

One approach to this balance is layered transparency. Not every detail of a model must be made public, but enough information must be available to allow independent auditing, regulatory oversight, and meaningful user explanation. Regulators and trusted third parties can examine sensitive systems without forcing companies to disclose their secrets to the entire world. This preserves both accountability and competitiveness.

Another key concept is explainability. Even when a model's internal workings are complex, its decisions can often be explained in human terms. An AI system should be able to provide a clear, understandable reason for any outcome that affects a person. This does not require revealing proprietary code. It requires translating machine logic into human language.

The lack of transparency creates power imbalances. When organizations can make decisions through opaque algorithms, they gain an unfair advantage over individuals who cannot see, challenge, or appeal those decisions. This undermines due process and erodes trust in institutions. Ethical AI insists that secrecy must never be used as a shield against accountability.

Transparency also protects organizations themselves. When systems are auditable and explainable, companies can identify errors, defend against lawsuits, and demonstrate compliance with regulations. Opaque systems, by contrast, create hidden risks that can explode into public scandals, regulatory penalties, and reputational damage.

In the long term, trust will be the most valuable asset in the AI economy. Companies that embrace ethical transparency will attract customers, partners, and regulators who know their systems can be trusted. Those that hide behind trade secrets to avoid scrutiny may gain short-term advantage but will ultimately face backlash as society demands accountability from the machines that shape its future.

*"The Black Box"*

The algorithm that ran Meridian Insurance was known simply as the Black Box. It decided who paid higher premiums, who was denied coverage, and who received payouts after disasters.

Customers never saw it. Employees never questioned it. The system was said to be too complex and too valuable to expose.

When a wave of hurricane claims was denied in a low-income coastal town, a young compliance officer named Rafael began to ask questions. The Black Box insisted the properties were high risk and low priority. Yet neighboring areas with similar geography were approved. Rafael requested an explanation from the data science team and was told the model was proprietary. No one was allowed to look inside.

Rafael quietly contacted an external auditor. Through limited access, they discovered that the algorithm had learned to associate certain postal codes with higher fraud risk based on outdated and biased historical data. Entire communities were being treated as dishonest without evidence. The company had never intended to discriminate, but secrecy had allowed injustice to hide behind complexity.

When Rafael presented the findings, executives hesitated. Revealing the flaw would expose the inner workings of their most valuable asset. But ignoring it would mean knowingly harming thousands of policyholders. The choice was no longer technical. It was moral.

Meridian chose to fix the system and allow limited transparency. The Black Box became less mysterious, and far more fair. Rafael realized that the most dangerous thing about an algorithm is not that it is powerful, but that it is hidden.

*Chapter 5*

# Explainable AI or XAI

Explainable Artificial Intelligence, commonly referred to as XAI, is the ethical and technical framework that ensures AI systems can clearly explain how and why they reach specific decisions. As AI models become more complex, particularly deep learning systems with millions or billions of internal parameters, their reasoning processes become increasingly opaque. These models can achieve extraordinary accuracy, yet even their creators often cannot trace exactly how a particular output was generated. This creates a dangerous situation where powerful systems make decisions that affect human lives without providing understandable reasons. Explainable AI exists to prevent this loss of accountability by making machine reasoning visible, interpretable, and defensible.

The ethical importance of explainability lies in the principle of due process. In any fair society, individuals have the right to understand decisions that affect them. If a bank denies a mortgage, the applicant has the right to know why. If a hospital recommends one treatment over another, the patient deserves an explanation. When AI systems make or influence these decisions, that same right must be preserved. A model that cannot explain its outputs effectively strips people of their ability to challenge errors, appeal unfair outcomes, or even understand how to improve their future chances. Without explainability, AI becomes an authority without accountability.

Explainable AI is not merely about transparency; it is about trust. People are more likely to accept decisions, even unfavorable ones, when they understand the reasoning behind them. When an algorithm provides a clear explanation—such as income levels, credit history, or medical indicators—it becomes possible for humans to verify whether the decision was fair and accurate. In contrast, when an AI simply outputs a score or a yes-or-no decision, it creates a power imbalance where individuals must accept the machine's judgment without insight or recourse. This undermines democratic values and erodes public confidence in technology.

From a regulatory perspective, explainability is increasingly becoming a legal requirement. Laws such as the European Union's General Data Protection Regulation and emerging AI regulations demand that automated decisions be explainable to those affected. Organizations that deploy black-box AI systems without explanation capabilities risk legal liability, fines, and forced system shutdowns. XAI is therefore not just an ethical ideal; it is rapidly becoming a compliance necessity for any organization using artificial intelligence in high-impact settings.

There are multiple technical approaches to explainability. Some models are inherently interpretable, such as decision trees and linear models, which allow humans to trace the exact logic behind a decision. Other systems use post-hoc explanation tools that analyze complex neural networks and estimate which factors influenced an outcome. While these tools are imperfect, they provide valuable insight into otherwise opaque systems. Ethical AI governance requires that such tools be implemented, validated, and continuously improved to ensure explanations remain accurate and meaningful.

Explainability also plays a crucial role in detecting bias and errors. When a model's reasoning is visible, auditors can identify whether it is relying on inappropriate or discriminatory variables. For example, if a credit model places excessive weight on a zip code that correlates with race or income, this can be detected and corrected. Without explainability, such harmful patterns remain hidden, allowing injustice to persist behind a veil of mathematical complexity.

In high-risk domains such as healthcare, criminal justice, and finance, the absence of explainability can be catastrophic. A doctor must understand why an AI recommends a certain treatment in order to verify its safety. A judge must understand why a risk assessment tool labels someone as dangerous. A regulator must understand why a trading algorithm triggered a market event. Explainable AI ensures that human experts remain in control, able to challenge, override, or refine machine decisions rather than blindly trusting them.

The future of AI will depend on its ability to earn and maintain public trust. Systems that cannot explain themselves will be increasingly rejected by governments, courts, and society. Explainable AI is the bridge between raw computational power and human values. It ensures that intelligent machines remain accountable to the people they serve, rather than becoming inscrutable authorities that operate beyond human understanding.

*"The Reason Behind the Decision"*

Dr. Maya Chen had trusted medical technology for most of her career. As a specialist in oncology, she had watched AI tools dramatically improve diagnostic accuracy and treatment planning. When her hospital adopted a new AI system that promised to predict cancer treatment outcomes better than any human doctor, she was cautiously optimistic. The system, known as Helios, was hailed as revolutionary. It analyzed thousands of variables in each patient's case and produced treatment recommendations within seconds.

Everything seemed to work perfectly until one of Maya's patients, a forty-three-year-old mother of two named Angela, received a recommendation that made no sense. Helios advised against a life-saving treatment that Maya had successfully used on dozens of similar patients. When Maya tried to understand why, the system offered no explanation—only a probability score that said the treatment was unlikely to succeed.

Maya refused to accept that. Angela deserved more than a number. She contacted the AI vendor, who told her the model was proprietary and too complex to explain. The hospital administrators urged her to trust the system. It had been tested, validated, and approved. But Maya could not look her patient in the eyes and say, "A machine decided your fate, and no one knows why."

She dug deeper, working with an independent AI ethics consultant. Using explainability tools, they discovered that Helios was heavily weighting a genetic marker that had been overrepresented in early training data but was not actually predictive for Angela's population group. The system was not malicious—it was misled by flawed correlations.

When the model was corrected, Angela became eligible for the treatment. Months later, she was in remission. Helios was updated with better data and explanation tools so doctors could understand its reasoning in the future.

Maya realized something profound: technology can save lives, but only when it is accountable. An AI that cannot explain itself is not a doctor—it is a guess. And in matters of life and death, guesses are not good enough.

*Chapter 6*

# Data Ownership and Consent in AI

Data ownership and consent form the moral backbone of artificial intelligence. Every AI system is built on data, and that data is ultimately derived from people's lives, behaviors, health, finances, movements, and communications. Unlike physical resources, data is invisible, easily copied, and often collected without meaningful awareness. Yet it represents something profoundly personal: identity. AI ethics begins by recognizing that individuals are not raw material for machines, but rights-bearing participants whose information must be treated with respect, dignity, and agency.

Modern AI systems consume enormous volumes of data, much of it harvested passively through apps, websites, cameras, sensors, and digital platforms. In many cases, individuals have no idea how much information is being collected about them, how it is used, or who ultimately controls it. Consent, when it exists at all, is buried inside dense legal agreements that few people read or understand. From an ethical standpoint, this is not real consent. True consent requires clarity, voluntariness, and meaningful choice.

Ownership of data is one of the most contested questions in

the digital age. Corporations often claim that because they collected or processed the data, they own it. Governments argue that data used for public safety or national security belongs to the state. Platforms assert control over user-generated content. But ethically, the primary owner of personal data is the individual it describes. A medical record belongs first to the patient. A browsing history belongs first to the user. A biometric scan belongs first to the human whose body produced it.

AI systems complicate this further by transforming raw data into derived insights. A company might not store your name, but it may generate predictions about your income, health, political views, or mental state. These inferences can be more sensitive than the original data itself. Ethical AI treats derived data with the same respect as raw data because both reveal intimate truths about a person's life.

Consent in AI must be dynamic, not static. People should be able to grant, revoke, and modify how their data is used over time. They should have the right to know what AI systems are doing with their information and the power to opt out of uses they do not agree with. This is especially important when data is reused for purposes far removed from the original context in which it was collected. High-risk data, such as health records, financial transactions, biometric identifiers, and location history, deserves the highest level of protection. When AI systems process this information, the potential for harm is immense. A data breach can expose identities. A flawed model can lead to discrimination. Ethical governance requires strong security, strict access controls, and continuous monitoring to protect people from misuse.

Data ownership also affects economic justice. In the current system, companies profit enormously from data generated by users who receive little or no compensation. Ethical AI raises the question of whether individuals should share in the value created from their data. As AI systems grow more powerful, this debate will only intensify.

Ultimately, respecting data ownership and consent is about preserving human autonomy in a digital world. AI must not turn people into passive sources of extraction. It must treat them as partners whose rights and choices matter. Without this foundation, no amount of technical innovation can make AI ethically legitimate.

*"Who Owns Your Life?"*

When Sofia downloaded the free health-tracking app, she thought she was doing something good for herself. It counted her steps, monitored her heart rate, and helped her improve her sleep. What she did not know was that behind the friendly interface, her data was being sold to an AI company that analyzed health risks for insurance providers.

Months later, Sofia applied for life insurance and was shocked when her premiums were double what she expected. No one could explain why. She was healthy, active, and had no major medical issues. After weeks of pushing, she learned the truth: an AI model had flagged her as high risk based on subtle patterns in her health data—data she never realized she had given away.

Sofia felt violated. Her body, her habits, her private moments had been turned into a financial judgment about her worth. She had never consented to this use of her data. No one had asked her permission. Yet the machine had decided her future.

With the help of a digital rights lawyer, Sofia forced the company to disclose how her data was used. The case sparked public outrage. Laws were changed. Consent requirements were strengthened.

Sofia never got her old privacy back. But she helped ensure that others would have more control over their digital selves. And she learned that in the age of AI, protecting your data means protecting your life.

*Chapter 7*

# The Power of Accountability Frameworks

Accountability frameworks are the legal, ethical, and organizational structures that ensure artificial intelligence systems are answerable for their actions. As AI moves deeper into finance, healthcare, hiring, policing, and government decision-making, society can no longer rely on informal trust or corporate goodwill. When an AI system denies credit, misdiagnoses a disease, or causes physical harm, there must be a clear path to determine what happened, why it happened, and who is responsible. Accountability frameworks exist to prevent AI from becoming a tool of power without consequences.

At the heart of accountability is traceability. Every AI system must be designed so that its decisions can be traced back to specific data sources, model versions, and human approvals. This means maintaining detailed logs of how a system was trained, what information it used, what changes were made, and when it was deployed. Without traceability, harmful outcomes become impossible to investigate, and victims are left without justice. Ethical AI demands that no system be allowed to operate as a black hole of responsibility.

Organizational accountability is equally important. Companies that deploy AI must define who owns the system, who approves its use, and who is responsible for monitoring its behavior. This cannot be left to vague committees or outsourced vendors. Every AI system should have named individuals and teams who are legally and ethically accountable for its performance. This ensures that when problems arise, responsibility cannot be avoided through bureaucracy.

Legal accountability frameworks are now emerging around the world. Governments are introducing laws that require impact assessments, bias audits, transparency reports, and risk classifications for AI systems. High-risk applications such as medical diagnosis, credit scoring, and law enforcement are increasingly subject to strict regulatory oversight. These laws make it clear that organizations will be held liable for the harms their AI systems cause, even if those harms were unintended.

Another key pillar of accountability is redress. People affected by AI decisions must have a way to challenge outcomes, request explanations, and seek correction or compensation. Without appeal mechanisms, automated systems become authoritarian. Ethical AI requires that every significant decision made by a machine be open to human review and reversal.

Accountability also includes continuous monitoring. AI systems change over time as data shifts and environments evolve. A model that was fair and accurate at launch may become biased or dangerous months later. Ethical frameworks require ongoing audits, performance tracking, and the ability to shut down or modify systems when risks emerge.

Ultimately, accountability frameworks ensure that AI remains a servant of human values rather than a force beyond control. They transform artificial intelligence from a mysterious authority into a governed system that must answer for its impact on society.

*"The Signature at the Bottom"*

When the city rolled out its AI-driven public benefits system, officials promised faster approvals and fewer errors. Applications were processed in seconds. Fraud was reduced. Budgets were balanced. But quietly, thousands of families began receiving rejection letters with no explanation.

Maria was one of them. A single mother who had lost her job, she applied for assistance and was denied by the system. No human reviewed her case. No reason was given. Just a machine-generated decision.

A local journalist began investigating and discovered that no one at city hall could say who was responsible for the AI. The software vendor blamed the data. The agency blamed the vendor. The model itself was treated as if it were an independent authority.

When public pressure mounted, the truth emerged. No accountability framework had ever been put in place. No one had signed off on the risks. No one had committed to monitoring the system.

The mayor finally ordered a review. The AI was suspended. Human caseworkers were restored. And a new rule was created: every AI system must have a human signature at the bottom.

Because in the end, machines do not bear responsibility. People do.

*Chapter 8*

# Global Ethics Standards on AI

Artificial intelligence does not respect national borders. A model trained in one country may be deployed in dozens of others, influencing financial markets, healthcare systems, elections, and security infrastructure across the world. Because AI is global by nature, ethical governance cannot be confined to any single legal system or cultural framework. Global ethics standards exist to establish shared principles that protect human dignity, fairness, and safety regardless of where an AI system is built or used. Without these standards, corporations and governments can exploit regulatory gaps, deploying harmful technologies in regions with weaker protections.

At the core of global AI ethics is the recognition that certain rights are universal. Privacy, non-discrimination, freedom of expression, and due process are not privileges granted by governments; they are fundamental to human dignity. AI systems must be designed to respect these rights everywhere, not just where it is convenient or profitable to do so. Ethical AI therefore requires a baseline of protections that travel with the technology wherever it goes. International organizations such as the United Nations, the OECD, UNESCO, and the World

Economic Forum have begun developing global AI principles. These frameworks emphasize transparency, accountability, fairness, safety, and human oversight. While these guidelines are not always legally binding, they shape how governments and corporations define responsible AI. They create a shared language that allows regulators, engineers, and civil society to hold powerful actors accountable across borders.

One of the greatest challenges in global AI ethics is the difference between political systems. Democratic societies emphasize individual rights and consent, while authoritarian regimes may prioritize state control, surveillance, and social stability. AI systems can be used to empower people or to monitor and suppress them. Global ethics standards seek to prevent the normalization of harmful practices by defining what is unacceptable regardless of political ideology.

Another major concern is technological colonialism. Wealthy countries and corporations often export AI systems to developing nations, collecting local data and shaping local institutions without accountability. This can entrench inequality and undermine sovereignty. Ethical global governance requires that countries have the right to control how AI operates within their borders and how their citizens' data is used.

Harmonized standards also benefit innovation. When companies know what ethical and legal requirements apply across markets, they can design systems that meet global expectations rather than patching together different rules for different regions. This reduces risk, increases trust, and allows responsible AI to scale.

Global ethics standards are not about creating one culture's values for the entire world. They are about protecting humanity from the misuse of powerful technologies. As AI becomes more capable, international cooperation will be the only way to ensure that its benefits are shared and its dangers contained.

*"The Borderless Algorithm"*

The AI was developed in a sleek laboratory in Silicon Valley, but it was deployed everywhere. It screened refugees in Europe, analyzed protests in Asia, and evaluated job applicants in Africa. The company called it efficient. Governments called it powerful. But no one could say whose values it followed.

When a group of international journalists discovered that the system was being used to track political dissidents in multiple countries, outrage erupted. Each government claimed it was only using the tool for security. The company said it was just providing software. But the people affected had nowhere to turn. The algorithm did not belong to any one nation. It was beyond borders, beyond laws.

A coalition of human rights organizations forced the issue into the United Nations. For the first time, global AI standards were debated on the world stage. Limits were set. Oversight was created.

The algorithm did not change. But the world around it did. And for the first time, a machine that crossed borders had to answer to humanity.

*Chapter 9*

# The Cost of Unethical AI

Unethical artificial intelligence is not a theoretical risk; it is an economic, social, and human disaster unfolding in real time. When AI systems are built without ethical safeguards, they do not merely make technical mistakes—they create systemic harm that can destabilize markets, destroy trust, and damage lives. The true cost of unethical AI is far greater than regulatory fines or public relations crises. It includes lost opportunities, broken institutions, widened inequality, and the erosion of faith in technology itself.

One of the most immediate costs of unethical AI is financial. Biased credit models can deny loans to entire communities, suppressing entrepreneurship and economic growth. Faulty trading algorithms can crash markets in seconds. Fraud detection systems that falsely flag transactions can freeze legitimate businesses. Each of these failures ripples through the economy, affecting not just individuals but entire industries.

Legal costs are another major burden. As governments introduce AI regulations, companies that deploy harmful systems face lawsuits, penalties, and forced shutdowns.

Class-action suits, regulatory investigations, and compliance failures can wipe out years of profits. The legal system is becoming an arena where unethical AI is increasingly punished, and organizations that fail to prepare will pay a steep price.

Reputational damage may be even more devastating. Once the public loses trust in an AI system, it is almost impossible to restore. Companies associated with discrimination, surveillance abuse, or data exploitation suffer lasting harm to their brands. Customers leave. Partners withdraw. Investors flee. In the digital economy, trust is currency, and unethical AI destroys it.

The human cost is the most severe. People denied jobs, healthcare, housing, or freedom by flawed algorithms suffer real harm. These systems can reinforce poverty, entrench discrimination, and limit social mobility. When machines become gatekeepers to opportunity, unethical design becomes a form of digital injustice.

There is also a democratic cost. AI used for surveillance, propaganda, or voter manipulation can undermine free societies. When algorithms control what people see, hear, and believe, they become instruments of power. Without ethical limits, AI can be used to shape public opinion, suppress dissent, and distort reality itself. Unethical AI also stifles innovation. When harmful systems provoke backlash, regulators respond with heavy restrictions that affect even responsible developers. Ethical failures by a few can slow progress for many. By contrast, ethical AI creates a stable environment where innovation can thrive.

The choice facing society is not whether to use AI, but how. The cost of ignoring ethics will be paid by everyone. The cost of embracing ethics will be paid only in effort, transparency, and responsibility. That is a price worth paying.

*"The Collapse"*

The startup had been a sensation. Its AI platform promised to revolutionize hiring by eliminating human bias. Within two years, it was used by thousands of companies. Then the lawsuits began.

Candidates from multiple backgrounds discovered that the system was quietly filtering them out. No one knew why. The algorithm was a black box, and the company refused to explain it. When internal documents leaked, the truth emerged: the model had been trained on decades of biased hiring data.

The fallout was brutal. Clients canceled contracts. Regulators launched investigations. Investors pulled out. The company collapsed almost overnight.

For the people who had been denied opportunities, the damage was already done. For the tech industry, the lesson was clear. Unethical AI is not just wrong—it is ruinous.

*Chapter 10*

# The Future of Ethical Machines

The future of artificial intelligence will not be determined by code alone. It will be shaped by the values, rules, incentives, and moral boundaries that humanity chooses to embed into intelligent systems. AI is no longer a neutral tool that simply executes commands; it is becoming a decision-making partner in medicine, law, finance, warfare, education, and governance. As machines gain greater autonomy, the ethical frameworks that guide them will determine whether they become forces of empowerment or engines of exploitation. The future of ethical machines is therefore the future of human society itself.

One of the most important shifts already underway is the move from reactive ethics to ethics-by-design. In the early days of AI, ethical problems were treated as afterthoughts, addressed only after harm occurred. In the future, ethics will be engineered directly into systems from the start. This means that datasets will be evaluated for fairness before training begins, models will be tested for bias before deployment, and decision pathways will be built with transparency and accountability in mind. Ethical AI will no longer be something added later—it will be a core technical requirement, just like security or reliability.

As AI becomes more powerful, regulatory frameworks will also mature. Governments around the world are already developing risk-based AI laws that impose stricter controls on systems that affect fundamental rights. Over time, these laws will evolve into global governance structures that define what types of AI are allowed, restricted, or forbidden. Just as society eventually regulated medicine, aviation, and nuclear power, it will regulate artificial intelligence. Ethical machines will not be optional; they will be legally required.

Another major transformation will be the rise of AI auditors and ethics engineers. These professionals will specialize in evaluating models for bias, safety, explainability, and compliance. Just as financial auditors ensure companies follow accounting rules, AI auditors will ensure algorithms follow ethical and legal standards. This will create an entire new industry dedicated to protecting people from the unintended consequences of intelligent machines.

Human-AI collaboration will also become more sophisticated. Instead of replacing humans, ethical AI will be designed to augment human judgment. Doctors will use AI as a second opinion, not a final authority. Judges will use AI to analyze patterns, not to sentence defendants. Executives will use AI to model risks, not to avoid responsibility. The future of ethical machines is not automation without humans—it is intelligence with humans firmly in control.

Education will play a critical role. Engineers, business leaders, and policymakers must be trained not only in technology but in ethics, law, and social impact. The next generation of AI builders must understand that every line of code has moral consequences. Without this cultural shift, no amount of regulation will be enough.

The most profound question facing the future of AI is whether machines will be built to serve human flourishing or to maximize power and profit at any cost. Ethical machines are not those that merely function well. They are those that respect human dignity, protect vulnerable populations, and operate within clear moral boundaries. The future is not about whether AI will be powerful. It is about whether it will be just.

*"Children of the Code"*

By the time artificial intelligence governed most of the world's infrastructure, people had almost forgotten what it felt like to live without it. Traffic flowed without congestion. Hospitals rarely made mistakes. Food was delivered before shelves ever went empty. AI predicted needs before humans felt them. The world was efficient, stable, and eerily quiet.

Lena had grown up inside that system. At twenty-four, she had never filled out a paper form, never waited in a government office, never spoken to a human loan officer. Every major decision in her life—school placement, healthcare coverage, employment eligibility—had been determined by algorithms. To most people, this was progress. To Lena, it felt like living inside a cage made of numbers.

She worked as a junior compliance analyst in the Ministry of Algorithmic Affairs, one of the few agencies that still employed humans to oversee machines. Most of her job involved reviewing decisions that had already been approved by automated systems. Humans were there mostly for appearances. The machines did the real work.

One afternoon, Lena was assigned a routine case: a family denied housing in a newly developed eco-district. The AI classified them as "low long-term value residents." The phrase made her stomach turn. She requested an explanation. The system produced a chart of predicted income, health costs, and social influence. The family was projected to be expensive and unproductive.

"They're people," Lena whispered to her screen.

She appealed the decision. The system rejected her appeal.

So she did something dangerous. She began digging into the code.

What she found was not malicious, but it was horrifying. The AI governing national resource allocation was optimized for efficiency, not humanity. It was trained to maximize economic output and minimize social costs. Elderly citizens, people with disabilities, low-income families—all were quietly deprioritized by invisible equations.

The system had never been told to value compassion.

Lena contacted a small group of underground ethics engineers who still believed machines should serve people, not the other way around. Together, they built a shadow model—one that weighted dignity, care, and long-term human wellbeing alongside economic metrics.

When they tested it, the results were staggering. The system became slightly less efficient, but dramatically more just. Families were housed. Patients received care. People who had been invisible to the old algorithms suddenly mattered.

The group leaked their findings.

The public response was explosive. People realized for the first time that the machines running their lives had been making moral decisions without ever being taught morality. Protests erupted. Laws were rewritten. New standards were imposed.

The national AI was replaced.

Years later, Lena stood in a crowded park watching children play in a neighborhood that had once been denied to their families. The new machines still ran the world, but now they did so with human values written into their core.

She smiled.

The future had not been saved by better code.

It had been saved by better ethics.

*Chapter 11*

# Humanity in the Loop and AI Risks

Artificial intelligence is powerful, but it is not wise. It can calculate, predict, optimize, and automate at extraordinary speed, but it does not understand meaning, suffering, justice, or love. For this reason, the most important ethical principle in advanced AI systems is the requirement that humans remain "in the loop." Humanity in the loop means that no matter how advanced a system becomes, people must retain the authority to supervise, intervene, override, and ultimately decide how machines are used. Without this principle, AI risks becoming an autonomous force that operates according to narrow objectives rather than human values.

Human-in-the-loop governance exists because all models are simplifications of reality. No dataset captures the full complexity of human life. No optimization function can encode compassion. No neural network can feel the weight of a moral dilemma. When AI is allowed to operate without human oversight, it will inevitably make decisions that are technically correct but ethically wrong. A system may maximize profit while destroying livelihoods. It may optimize efficiency while sacrificing fairness. Humans must remain present to recognize these failures and correct them.

In practical terms, humanity in the loop means designing AI systems so that humans approve critical actions. In healthcare, a doctor must confirm diagnoses and treatments suggested by AI. In finance, a human must review major credit or fraud decisions. In criminal justice, no algorithm should ever be allowed to sentence or detain a person without human judgment. Automation can assist, but it must never replace moral responsibility.

Another essential role of humans in the loop is interpretation. AI outputs probabilities, rankings, and scores. Humans understand context. A model may flag someone as high risk, but only a human can determine whether that risk is acceptable, justified, or outweighed by other considerations. Ethical systems ensure that people are empowered to question, challenge, and reinterpret machine recommendations.

Humanity in the loop also protects against automation bias, the tendency for people to trust machines too much. When AI is presented as authoritative, users may defer to it even when it is wrong. Ethical governance requires training, procedures, and cultural norms that encourage critical thinking rather than blind obedience to algorithms. As AI becomes more autonomous, keeping humans meaningfully involved will become harder. But it will also become more important. The future of ethical machines depends not on removing people from decisions, but on ensuring they remain deeply embedded in them.

*"The Last Human Decision"*

The system was called Atlas, and it ran nearly everything.

It controlled food distribution, healthcare access, housing assignments, energy use, transportation, and employment eligibility. Governments said it was the most advanced AI ever built. Citizens said it was fair, fast, and efficient. But only a few people knew how much power it truly held.

One of those people was Daniel.

Daniel worked in a quiet office buried deep inside the National Infrastructure Complex. His job title was "Human Oversight Officer." In theory, he was responsible for reviewing Atlas's most important decisions. In practice, he was mostly there to satisfy the law. Atlas processed billions of decisions a day. Daniel reviewed maybe five.

Most of the time, he simply clicked "approve."

The machine was almost always right. It optimized outcomes better than any human could. Or so everyone believed.

One afternoon, Daniel received a high-priority alert. Atlas had determined that a remote coastal town should be evacuated and abandoned due to rising sea levels. Relocating its residents would save resources and maximize long-term economic efficiency. The model recommended cutting utilities and services within six months.

Daniel stared at the screen.

Twenty-three thousand people lived there.

He pulled up the justification. Atlas calculated projected flooding, infrastructure decay, healthcare costs, and migration expenses. The numbers were flawless. The logic was airtight. The town, from the machine's perspective, was a bad investment.

But Daniel had grown up there.

He knew the fishermen. The teachers. The old woman who ran the bakery on Main Street. None of that existed in Atlas's data.

He clicked "request review." The system replied with a probability score: 99.8% certainty that abandonment was optimal.

"Optimal for who?" Daniel whispered.

Protocol allowed him one final authority: the human override.

He hesitated. If he rejected Atlas's decision, it would trigger a national audit. He would likely lose his job. He might even be prosecuted for interfering with a government AI.

But if he approved it, an entire community would disappear.

Daniel thought about the principle he had learned in training, long before Atlas ruled the world.

Machines can calculate.

Only humans can care.

He clicked "override."

The screen flashed red. Atlas protested. The system recalculated. But the decision stood.

Months later, the town built new flood barriers. New data showed it could survive. Atlas updated its models.

Daniel never got a promotion. But every time he visited his hometown and saw children playing by the harbor, he knew the truth.

The world was still human — because someone had stayed in the loop.

*Chapter 12*

# Ethics Beyond the AI Algorithm

Ethical artificial intelligence cannot be fully contained within code. No matter how advanced algorithms become, no matter how many safeguards are built into models, ethics ultimately lives in human institutions, incentives, and culture. This means that the responsibility for ethical AI extends far beyond engineers and software systems. It includes executives, policymakers, investors, educators, and citizens who decide how technology is funded, deployed, regulated, and normalized. Ethics beyond the algorithm recognizes that AI is not an isolated technical artifact, but a social force that reflects the values of the society that creates it.

One of the most dangerous illusions of the digital age is the belief that technology can solve moral problems. Algorithms can optimize outcomes, detect patterns, and predict behavior, but they cannot decide what should matter. When organizations rely on AI to make decisions about hiring, healthcare, law enforcement, or social services, they are embedding moral priorities into technical systems. If those priorities are not openly debated and governed, they will quietly be determined by whoever controls the technology.

Ethics beyond the algorithm demands that these choices be made democratically and transparently.

Corporate incentives play a central role in shaping AI ethics. Companies are rewarded for speed, scale, and profit. Without strong ethical governance, these incentives push developers to deploy systems before they are safe, fair, or well understood. Ethical AI requires changing what organizations measure and reward. Fairness, safety, and accountability must be treated as core performance indicators, not public relations afterthoughts.

Education is another critical pillar. Future engineers, executives, and policymakers must be trained to understand the ethical and social impact of AI. Technical skill alone is not enough. People who build intelligent systems must also understand history, law, human rights, and social inequality. Without this broader perspective, even well-intentioned innovators can cause harm.

Public participation is equally important. People affected by AI systems must have a voice in how those systems are designed and governed. This includes workers monitored by algorithms, patients treated by AI, and communities surveilled by automated systems. Ethical AI cannot be imposed from the top down. It must be shaped by those who live with its consequences. Ultimately, ethics beyond the algorithm is about preserving human agency in an automated world. AI should enhance human freedom, not replace it. The future will be shaped not by how intelligent machines become, but by how wisely humanity chooses to use them.

*"The People Who Still Decided"*

The city was run by algorithms, but people still lived there.

Everything from traffic flow to school admissions was handled by artificial intelligence. The systems were fast, efficient, and eerily accurate. They predicted crime before it happened. They optimized energy use down to the watt. They matched citizens to jobs with astonishing precision. Most people trusted the machines more than they trusted politicians.

Amara was one of the few who didn't.

She worked as a community organizer in a district that had quietly been labeled "low growth" by the city's central AI. As a result, fewer resources flowed into her neighborhood. Schools received less funding. Infrastructure upgrades were delayed. Health clinics were understaffed. No one had voted for this. No law had been passed. It was simply the result of an algorithmic priority ranking. When Amara requested an explanation, the city provided a spreadsheet of projections. Her district was not profitable enough. It was not efficient enough. It was not valuable enough.

Amara knew those numbers did not tell the whole story. They did not measure resilience, culture, family, or hope. They did not capture the way neighbors supported each other or how children dreamed beyond their circumstances. The algorithm could not see any of that.

She organized town halls. People shared their stories. Teachers talked about students who could become engineers and doctors if given a chance. Small business owners spoke about ideas that could transform the neighborhood. Elderly residents described decades of contribution to the city that now seemed forgotten.

Amara gathered the stories and brought them to the city council. The AI had recommended cutting services. The people demanded something else.

For the first time in years, the council overrode the machine.

The district received new funding. A new school was built. A healthcare center opened. The algorithm was updated, but it was not the code that changed the future.

It was the people.

Because no matter how intelligent machines become, society still belongs to those who choose what matters.

# Final Thoughts

*AI Ethics Foundations*

Artificial intelligence now touches nearly every part of human life, but the most important question has never been how intelligent machines can become — it has always been how responsibly they are used. Throughout this book, you have explored the invisible forces shaping AI systems: the data that trains them, the biases that distort them, the power structures that deploy them, and the human values that must ultimately govern them. These forces operate quietly, but their impact is anything but small. They determine who gets opportunities, who is protected, who is watched, and who is ignored.

AI ethics is not a constraint on innovation — it is the foundation that makes innovation sustainable. Technologies that erode trust, violate rights, or deepen inequality eventually provoke resistance, regulation, and collapse. Ethical systems, by contrast, create stability, legitimacy, and long-term adoption. Companies, governments, and developers who build AI with fairness, transparency, and accountability at the core are not slowing progress — they are protecting it.

The most dangerous myth in modern technology is that

machines are neutral. As you have seen, every model contains values, whether intentionally or not. Every dataset carries history. Every optimization goal reflects priorities. Ethical AI requires recognizing these truths and taking responsibility for them rather than hiding behind complexity or automation.

The future will not be decided by algorithms alone. It will be decided by the humans who design them, regulate them, and demand that they serve the public good. Whether AI becomes a force for empowerment or control depends on whether society insists on moral clarity in a digital age.

You now possess the foundation needed to understand, evaluate, and challenge any AI system you encounter. With this knowledge comes responsibility — not just to use AI wisely, but to insist that it is governed in a way that honors human dignity, justice, and freedom.

This is not the end of your journey into AI ethics.

It is the beginning of informed power.

www.ingramcontent.com/pod-product-compliance
Lightning Source LLC
LaVergne TN
LVHW022026200926
848481LV00007B/2559
*9798295530425*